USING THIS BOOK

Children learn to read by ***reading****, but they need help to begin with.*

When you have read the story on the left-hand pages aloud to the child, go back to the beginning of the book and look at the pictures together.

Encourage children to read the sentences under the pictures. If they don't know a word, give them a chance to 'guess' what it is from the illustrations, before telling them.

There are more suggestions for helping children to learn to read in the *Parent/Teacher* booklet.

British Library Cataloguing in Publication Data

McCullagh, Sheila K.
The Gruffle in Puddle Lane.—(Puddle Lane reading programme. Stage 3; v. 3)
I. Title II. Dillow, John III. Series
823'.914[J] PZ7

ISBN 0-7214-0935-0

First edition

Published by Ladybird Books Ltd Loughborough Leicestershire UK
Ladybird Books Inc Lewiston Maine 04240 USA

The Gruffle in Puddle Lane

written by SHEILA McCULLAGH
illustrated by JOHN DILLOW

This book belongs to:

____

Ladybird Books

The Gruffle was a gruff and
grumpy monster.
He was **very** grumpy, and
he was **very** gruff.
He didn't often come to the garden
of the old house in Puddle Lane,
but when he did, everyone was careful
not to make him cross.
The difficulty was, that the Gruffle
could vanish whenever he wanted to.
And if he was invisible, no one
could see him.
But when they **did** see the Gruffle
in the garden, everyone tried
to be very quiet and careful.

The Gruffle was
a gruff and grumpy monster.
He was **very** grumpy,
and he was **very** gruff.

A blackbird lived in a tree in the garden
of the old house.
The blackbird liked to sing
every morning.
But he never sang, if he saw the Gruffle.
The Gruffle didn't like to hear
anyone singing.

A blackbird lived in a tree
in the garden.
The blackbird liked to sing.

An owl lived in the attic
of the old house.
He often hooted, as he flew
out of the window.
"To-whit to-whoo!"
But he always flew silently away,
if he saw the Gruffle.
The Gruffle didn't like to hear
anyone hooting.

An owl lived in the attic.
The owl liked to hoot.

One day, very early in the morning,
the Gruffle was in the garden
of the old house.
The owl saw the Gruffle,
as he flew home to the attic,
and he was careful not to hoot.
The blackbird was up, but he didn't sing.
He sat on a branch
and watched the Gruffle.
The Gruffle went to the garden gate.
He looked through the gate
into Puddle Lane.
There was no one about.
The Gruffle opened the gate,
and went into the lane.

One day, the Gruffle
was out in the garden.
He opened the gate, and
went into Puddle Lane.

Old Mr Gotobed woke up early
in his house in Puddle Lane.
He didn't feel very well,
so he didn't get dressed.
He went downstairs, and made a cup of
tea, and took the tea back to bed.
But the milk had gone sour.
When old Mr Gotobed tasted his tea,
it wasn't right at all.
Old Mr Gotobed opened his window.

He made a cup of tea.
The tea was not right.
Mr Gotobed opened his window.

The Gruffle was in the lane,
just under Mr Gotobed's window.
Only the Gruffle's ears were showing.
The rest of him was invisible.
Mr Gotobed wouldn't have seen him,
even if he had looked out of the window.
But he didn't look out of the window.
He tossed out the tea without looking.
Swoosh!
The tea fell on the Gruffle's head.

Mr Gotobed tossed the tea
out of the window –
Swoosh!
The tea fell on the Gruffle's head.

The Gruffle roared.
He gave a great roar of rage,
and came into view.
He stood there in the lane, under
Mr Gotobed's window.
Mr Gotobed could see him now.
He could hear him, too, for the Gruffle
roared again.
"I'm dreaming!" cried Mr Gotobed.
"I'm having a nightmare.
I must be still asleep.
I'll go back to bed!"

Mr Gotobed saw the Gruffle.
The Gruffle roared.

Mr Gotobed ran back to his bed.
He climbed in and pulled the sheet
over his head.
The Gruffle roared again.
He went off down the lane,
feeling crosser than ever.
Mr Gotobed put his fingers in his ears,
and stayed under the sheet.

Mr Gotobed ran back to bed.
The Gruffle roared again,
and went down the lane.

Mr Puffle got up early that morning.
He was feeling very cheerful.
Mr Puffle began to sing.
He picked up his watering can and opened his window, to water the flowers in the window box outside.

Mr Puffle got up.
He began to sing.
Mr Puffle opened his window.
He picked up his watering can.

But the Gruffle was in the lane.
Just at that moment, the Gruffle went
by Mr Puffle's house.
He heard Mr Puffle singing, and
he looked up with a roar of rage.
Mr Puffle looked out, and saw the Gruffle.
Mr Puffle was so surprised,
that he dropped the watering can.

The Gruffle was in the lane.
Mr Puffle dropped
the watering can.

The watering can fell
on the Gruffle's head.
The Gruffle roared and roared again.
Then he vanished.

The watering can fell
on the Gruffle's head.

Mr Puffle shut the window quickly,
and put his hand in front of his eyes.
"There's nothing there,"
he said to himself.
"I just imagined it. Or else
I ate too much supper last night,
and I'm not very well."

Mr Puffle shut the window.

He opened his fingers, and looked through them.
He looked out of the window.
There was no one in the lane.
The Gruffle had vanished.
Mr Puffle gave a great sigh.
"Just as I thought," he said.
"There's nothing there. I imagined it."
But he locked the window, and he didn't open it again that day.

Mr Puffle looked out of the window.
There was no one in the lane.

Mrs Pitter-Patter was sitting
in her front room, having breakfast.
She wasn't doing anything that would
make the Gruffle angry.
She was just having a cup of tea.
But by this time, the Gruffle was so cross,
that it made him angry just to see anyone.
The Gruffle looked in through the window,
and saw Mrs Pitter-Patter.
Only his ears were showing.
The rest of him was still invisible.
He was feeling very grumpy indeed,
and he didn't like the look of
Mrs Pitter-Patter at all.

Mrs Pitter-Patter was having
a cup of tea.
The Gruffle looked in at the
window.
He saw Mrs Pitter-Patter.

The Gruffle gave a great roar,
and all of him came into view.
He stood there at the window, looking in.
He roared loudly, and then
he roared again.

The Gruffle roared.
He roared and roared again.

Mrs Pitter-Patter looked up,
and saw a big, red monster looking
in at the window.
She dropped her cup, and fainted.

Mrs Pitter-Patter looked up.
She saw a big, red monster.

The Gruffle was just going to roar again, when he heard a little squeak behind him. He turned around, and saw a little mouse sitting in the middle of the lane.
The Gruffle's roar changed to a yell of fright.
There was only one thing the Gruffle was afraid of, and that was a mouse.

The Gruffle saw a little mouse,
sitting in the lane.

In a moment, the Gruffle had vanished.
He rushed back down the lane into the garden, and banged the gate behind him.
The little mouse ran up the wall of Mrs Pitter-Patter's house.
Her breakfast was still on the table.
The little mouse went in.

The Gruffle vanished.
He ran away, down the lane.
The little mouse went into
Mrs Pitter-Patter's house.

Mrs Pitter-Patter was lying back
in her chair.
The little mouse climbed up
on to the table and helped himself
to Mrs Pitter-Patter's breakfast.
Then he sat up, and combed his whiskers.
And then he left.

The little mouse sat on the table.

When Mrs Pitter-Patter woke up,
she looked all around the room,
but there was no one there.
Mrs Pitter-Patter made herself
a cup of tea.
And when she had drunk it,
she made herself another cup.
And then she made another.
She did nothing else for
the rest of the day.

Mrs Pitter-Patter woke up.
She made herself a cup of tea.

Have you read these stories? They are all about the people and characters who live in Puddle Lane?

Stage 2

5 The Gruffle

Stage 3

1 Old Mr Gotobed

5 The magic penny

the Gruffle

from Old Mr Gotobed